VOLCANO!

Ellen J. Prager

ILLUSTRATED BY Nancy Woodman

NATIONAL GEOGRAPHIC SOCIETY

Washington, D.C.

The rocky ground shakes and bulges upward. Then a powerful blast throws rock bombs, gas, and ash high into the sky. Fiery red lava pours from the Earth, and nearby fields of snow and ice melt, creating huge rivers of thick mud.

VOLCANO!

4

Some volcanoes lie quiet, asleep for many years.

TO THE MOUNTAIN

6

When a volcano sleeps,
beneath its rocky cover all is still and quiet.

7

Other volcanoes are more active and erupt more often. When a volcano wakes, hot liquid rock and gas go on the move. An exploding volcano is an awesome sight and dangerous for those living nearby.

Let's look more closely at how a volcano erupts by going inside its fiery underbelly.

Beneath the ground, melted rock is called magma. When it bursts out onto the Earth's surface, magma is then called lava.

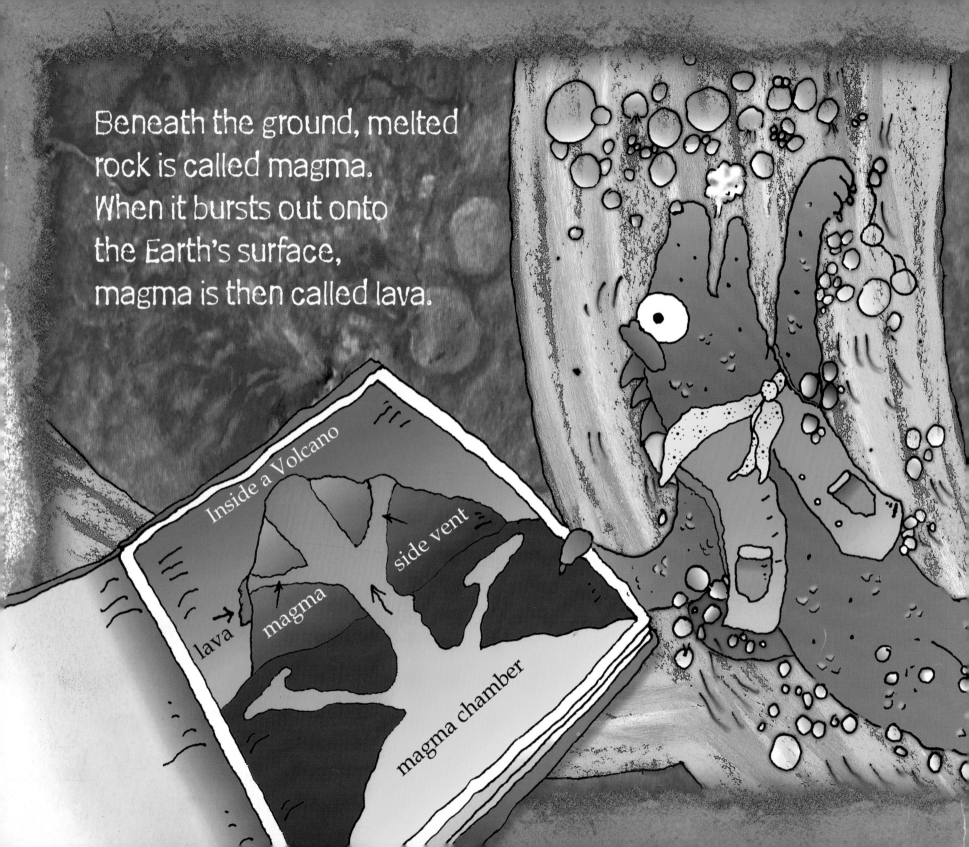

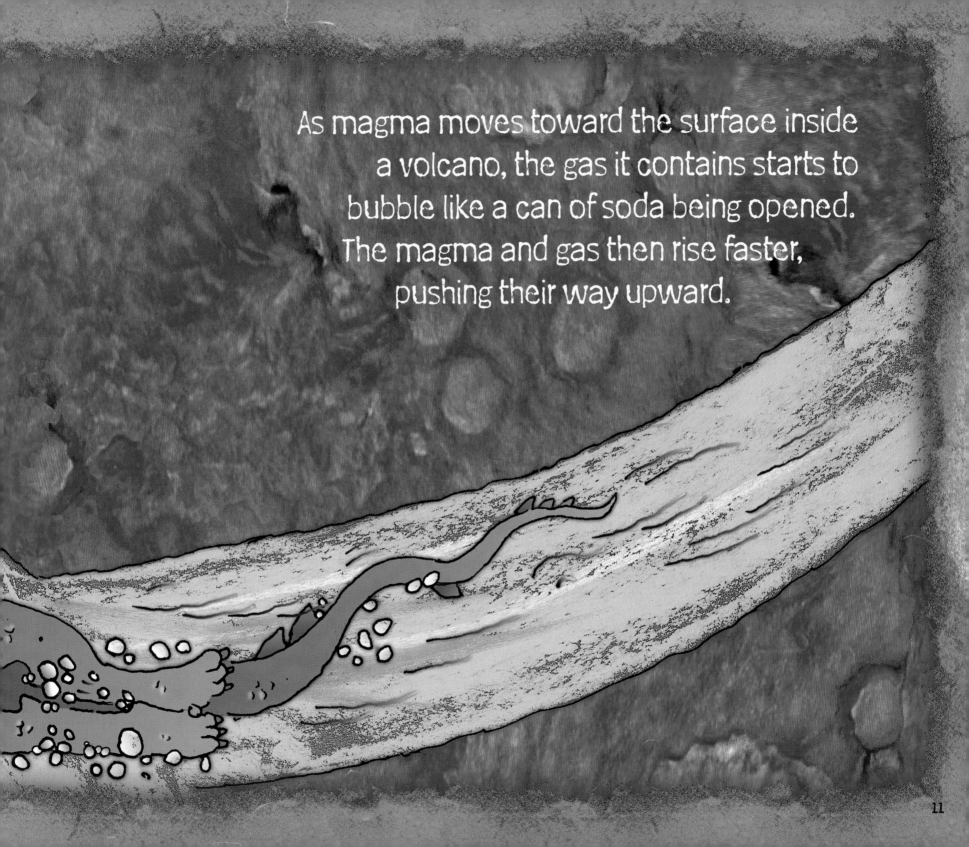

As magma moves toward the surface inside a volcano, the gas it contains starts to bubble like a can of soda being opened. The magma and gas then rise faster, pushing their way upward.

When magma begins to move upward beneath a volcano, the land rumbles and shakes. Earthquakes are often a sign that a volcano is active.

As gas and magma collect
below a volcano's rocky top, the
surface may begin to bulge outward.
Tall pillars of steam shoot skyward as
gas escapes through cracks and holes in the rock.

If too much magma
and gas build up, or if an
earthquake or landslide pops
the volcano's top, it erupts.

VOLCANO!

Often the first sign of an eruption is a huge towering cloud of gas and ash.

Thick clouds of ash block out the sun and turn daylight into darkness. Wind high above a volcano can spread the erupting gas and ash far away. And like a heavy gray snow, the ash falls to the ground and buries all below.

Along with gas and ash, sometimes big rock blocks, or bombs, are thrown out of a volcano's rumbling mouth. Glowing red blobs of lava may also be tossed high into the sky and fall to the ground, forming a giant black cinder cone.

Mud on the Move

In the most powerful and deadly eruptions, volcanoes unleash burning clouds of gas and ash that rush down their sides at superfast speeds.

If snow and ice cover the volcano, they may melt, mix with rock, and create dangerous mudflows.

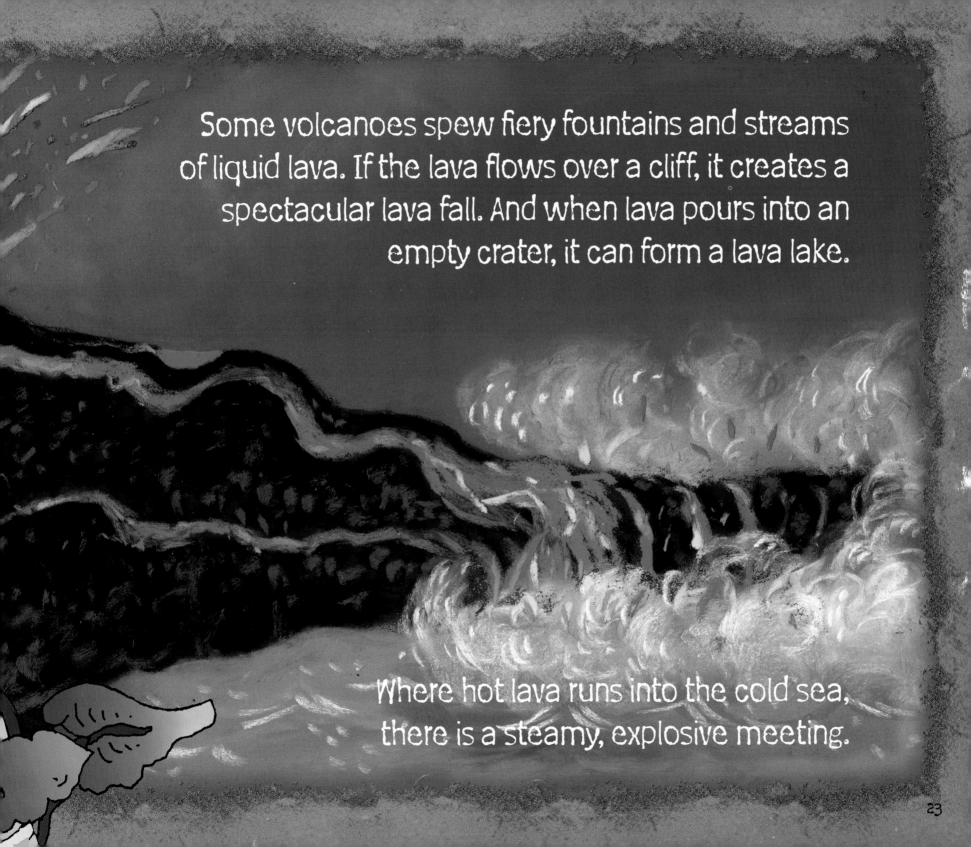

Some volcanoes spew fiery fountains and streams of liquid lava. If the lava flows over a cliff, it creates a spectacular lava fall. And when lava pours into an empty crater, it can form a lava lake.

Where hot lava runs into the cold sea, there is a steamy, explosive meeting.

When lava cools, it hardens into rock. In different places there are different kinds of lava rock depending on what the lava is made of and how it erupted.

In Hawaii there are two types of black lava rock. "Aa" (ahh-ahh) lava is rough and blocky, with very sharp edges. "Pahoehoe" (pah-hoy-hoy) lava looks smooth, like flowing, twisty ropes hardened into stone.

Lava Rock

Aa

Pahoehoe

Scientists study volcanoes all over the world. They want to predict how and when volcanoes will erupt and to warn people living nearby.

Mount Redoubt

Mount Mageik

Mount St. Helens

Hawaii

Iceland

NORTH AMERICA

Soufriere Hills Volcano

Nevado del Ruiz

ATLANTIC OCEAN

SOUTH AMERICA

PACIFIC OCEAN

VOLCANOES OF THE WORLD

🌋 = VOLCANIC AREA

Mt. Redoubt, Alaska

Mt. St. Helens, Washington

Soufriere Hills Volcano, Montserrat

Lava blast, Hawaii

Cinder cone, Iceland

Nevado del Ruiz, Colombia

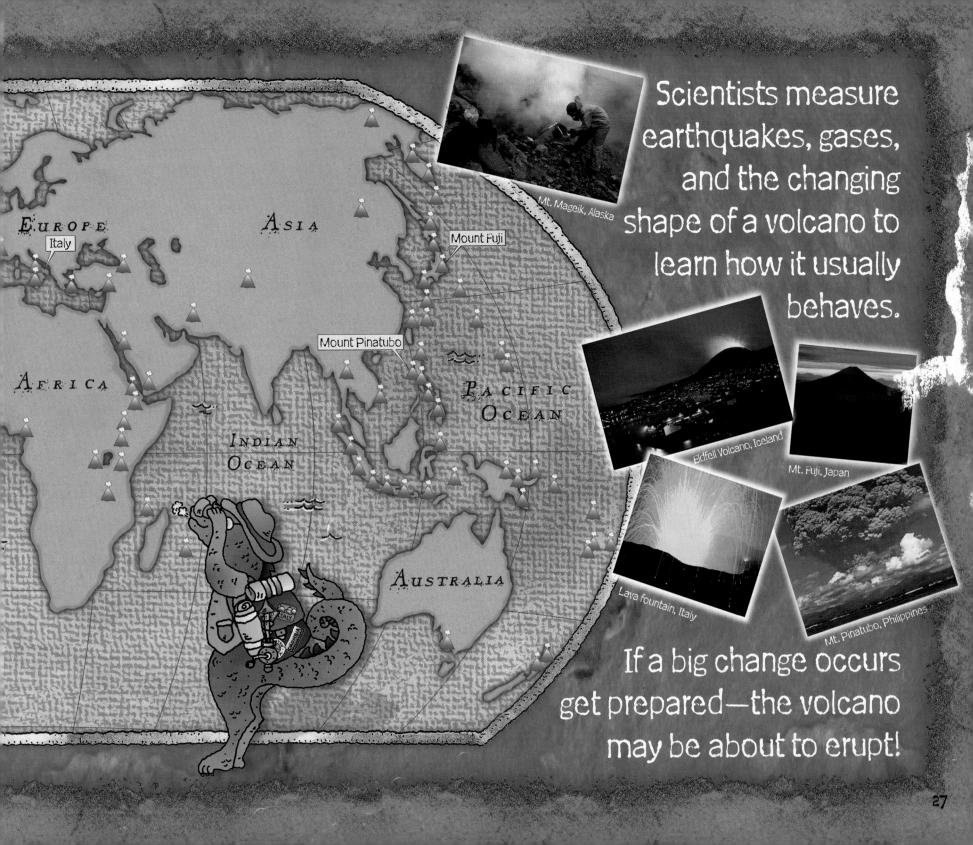

Scientists measure earthquakes, gases, and the changing shape of a volcano to learn how it usually behaves.

If a big change occurs get prepared—the volcano may be about to erupt!

EUROPE

Italy

ASIA

AFRICA

Mount Fuji

Mount Pinatubo

INDIAN OCEAN

PACIFIC OCEAN

AUSTRALIA

Mt. Mageik, Alaska

Eldfell Volcano, Iceland

Mt. Fuji, Japan

Lava fountain, Italy

Mt. Pinatubo, Philippines

Is there a VOLCANO sleeping near you?

Build your own VOLCANO!

Here's what you'll need:

- Newspaper
- A drinking straw
- A scoop
- Several cups of flour

1. Make a volcano-shaped mound of flour on the newspaper.

2. Use the straw to make a hole in the top of the volcano.

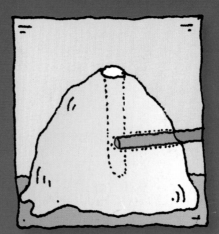

3. Clean out the straw. Stick it through the side of the volcano and into the center.

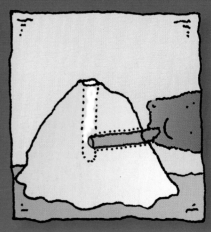

4. Blow very gently into the straw. Then blow a little harder.

What did you discover?

Just as in a real volcano, the height of the ash (dry flour) depended on the amount of force from below (you blowing), and where it went, on the flow of air (wind) over the volcano.

Use a mirror to read.

Just as volcano

The flour you blew is like an ash cloud.
What determines the height and direction of the ash?

The artwork in this book is a digital collage of pastels on
sandpaper and pastel paper, watercolors, and photographs.
The type for the book is set in Coventry.
Book design and character concept by Nancy Woodman

Jump Into Science Series Consultant:
Gary Brockman, Early Education Science Specialist

Printed in Mexico

Library of Congress Cataloging-in-Publication Data
Prager, Ellen J.
Volcano! / by Ellen J. Prager; illustrated by Nancy Woodman.
p. cm.
ISBN 0-7922-8201-9
1. Volcanoes—Juvenile literature. [1. Volcanoes.] I. Woodman, Nancy, ill.
II Title.
QE521.3.P73   2001
551.21—dc21   00-011928
PHOTOGRAPHY CREDITS: p. 2 Michael Quearry. p.4 AP/Wide World Photo. p. 16 Michael P.
Doukas, USGS. p. 20 left Daniel Dzurisin, USGS; right Lyn Topinka, USGS. p. 22 left David Gad-
dis; right USGS. p.25 left Robert Dashiell; right David Gaddis. pp. 24-25 lava beach detail
based on photo by Fred Hirschmann. p.26 (counterclockwise from top): USGS photo; Jim
Valance, USGS; Vincent J. Musi (NGS); Norm Banks, USGS; Robert Patton (NGS); Robert
Madden (NGS). p.27 (counterclockwise from top): Bea Ritchie, USGS; Robert Patton (NGS);
B. Chouet/USGS; Rick Hobbitt, USGS; George F. Mobley (NGS)

The world's largest nonprofit scientific and educational organization, the National Geographic Society was founded in 1888 "for the increase and diffusion of geographic knowledge." Since then it has supported
scientific exploration and spread information to its more than eight million members worldwide. The National Geographic Society educates and inspires millions every day through magazines, books, television
programs, videos, maps and atlases, research grants, the National Geographic Bee, teacher workshops, and innovative classroom materials. The Society is supported through membership dues, charitable gifts, and income
from the sale of its educational products. Members receive NATIONAL GEOGRAPHIC magazine—the Society's official journal—discounts on Society products, and other benefits. For more information about the
National Geographic Society, its educational programs, publications, or ways to support its work, please call 1-800-NGS-LINE (647-5463), or write to the following address: